MANAGING IN THE
DIGITAL ERA

Nuno Ribeiro

MANAGING IN THE
DIGITAL ERA

Nuno Ribeiro

Preface by Rui Pêgo

This book's sales profits will be donated to
CERCI Lisboa
Cooperativa de Educação e Reabilitação de Cidadãos Inadaptados, CRL

Published / 2011
Also available on ebook

www.managinginthedigitalera.com

Title: Managing in the Digital Era
Original Title: Gerir na Era Digital
Author: Nuno Ribeiro
Preface: Rui Pêgo
ISBN: 978-1466319219
Copyright: Nuno Ribeiro, 2011

Translation: Nazaré Carvalho (nazare.rcc@gmail.com)
Editing: Jonathan Epstein
Cover: Hugo Vicente
Pagination: José Galvão and Hugo Vicente
Technical support to the publishing: José Galvão
Photography: Rui Freire

Profits from the sale of this book donated to:
Cerci - Cooperativa de Educação e Reabilitação de Cidadãos Inadaptados
Av.ª Avelino Teixeira da Mota Lote E
1950-033 Lisboa
Portugal

Phone: (+351) 21 839 17 00
Fax: (+351) 21 859 87 48
Email: geral@cercilisboa.org.pt
Site: www.cercilisboa.org.pt

www.managinginthedigitalera.com
www.facebook.com/managinginthedigitalera

To my wife Sandra and my children Rodrigo and Sofia
To my parents, Carlos and Clementina
To my brother Rui

Contents

Introductory Note

In early 2008, Carla Ferreira Borges, editor-in-chief of Jornal Meios & Publicidade (The Journal of Media and Advertising), challenged me to write articles on how media is changing in the digital area. I accepted the challenge , and with Carla's agreement published the articles in my blog – Cibertransistor.com – to ensure that the articles would enjoy ongoing interaction with the readers and to keep a (living) digital archive.

For three years I have been collecting my ideas, reflections and analyses in (hyper)text for Meios & Publicidade and for Cibertransistor.com.

Looking back over these years, I realized that it would be worthwhile updating these texts and compiling and organizing them into this book, especially since there are on-line services that greatly facilitate and simplify this process. I decided to use Lulu.com service, that allowed me to publish both paper books and eBooks and to have a broader distribution. Thus, the decision to make this book was "spontaneous" and its publication "instantaneous".

I have decided to donate all the profits generated by the book to CERCI in Lisbon – the Cooperative of Education and Rehabilitation of Handicapped Citizens. The hectic daily lives many of us lead tend to make us forget that there are people, children and adults, who for various reasons face major difficulties in adapting to our society. Many institutions like CERCI have the mission to help these people and offer them a better life.

The technological evolution and the new Digital Era can also help many of those who look for the support of institutions like CERCI to expand their horizons, adapt their skills, or simply express themselves. As citizens, we can and should contribute to this social and solidarity mission. This was one of the ways I found to contribute. You, by buying and/or reading this book, are also contributing to this mission.

Acknowledgements

I would like to thank all of those with whom I had the opportunity to work, to discuss and reflect on the changes that technology, telecommunications and (new) media are bringing to societies.

I would like to give special thanks to:

- Carla Ferreira Borges, for having challenged me to write articles for Meios & Publicidade, the "embryo" of this book.

- The board of Controlinveste and all the elements of my team, for trusting me and for their commitment and dedication to our change management work throughout these last three years.

- Rui Pêgo, my friend and great communications professional, whom I have admired for a long time, and who accepted my request to write the preface to this book.

- Jonathan Epstein, one of the best digital media managers that I have worked with and also a friend, volunteered to do the editing of the english version.

Thank You
Nuno Ribeiro
Lisbon, January 5, 2011

Preface by Rui Pêgo

A world in continuous transformation, particularly in the beginning of a new Era, produces various (social) anguishes, (economic) perplexities, and fatal (corporate) ambiguities that can have terrifying impacts on our individual plans and on the ways we have become used to when relating with our surroundings.

These are the topics of Nuno Ribeiro's book. Both player in, and attentive observer of the changes we have been witnessing, he systematizes the tremendous complexity of the corporate and business redesign processes using language we can all understand, without ever giving in to the comfortable idea of "final". He even says, in the first chapter, that he "intends to reflect on the challenges and realities that we live with today," but notes that "tomorrow everything can change…".

In the "eye of the hurricane", the (traditional) media industry has been developing new initiatives, not always in the best way, but it has made decisions with some strategic impact that have allowed it to reconvert production models (if timidly) and adapt to the requirements of the current reality.

The (digital) environment in which we live and the changes it has brought to our media consumption patterns require that the traditional media (radio, television, press) make additional efforts to adapt to a multiplatform universe, in order to capture the various audiences that have progressively been shifting their attention and preferences to new venues, by utilizing both traditional and new media in an integrated way.

This new reality places the content offering (ideally diversified and differentiating) in the center of the business, places strategic value on filtering multiple segments of increasingly demanding consumers, and makes a multiplicity of distribution channels absolutely necessary. As such, the redesign of production pathways, to simplify the flow of content among platforms, the restructuring of organizations, and the recruiting of new competencies are essential to produce an adequate response for the media company to these different audiences with their combination of new needs and traditional consumption habits.

The old relationship between broadcaster and audience has been breached. Even though many of us still listen to music on the radio, watch television on the TV set, and are drawn to the intimacy of a paper newspaper, the audience's role is changing and moving toward the center of the media universe. It is the audience who chooses the broadcasters of news and entertainment and the most convenient times for those broadcasts. The audience produces its own content -- user-generated content -- and makes it freely available. Producing one's own content or participating in programming is not new (radio has for a long time relied on its listeners for content); the novelty is the capacity of the consumer audience to publish its content without relying on corporate "broadcasting centers".

We live in a world where newspapers use audio and video; mobile phones play music and are information centers; tablets are a seemingly endless source of information and entertainment, and where images of radio open the TV news. Content from various origins lives side by side in the same (digital) environment, competing for the attention of consumers, and creating a change in consumption habits. These days, less and less people will sit on the river bank watching the "river" go by, instead preferring the "lake", to quote Christian Nissen's inspired analogy, when he uses this language to refer to linear programming and downloadable content respectively. If this seeming trend is confirmed, more and more people will consume in a non-traditional way. Already, according to Havas, 33% of Internet consumers simultaneously listen to the radio while consuming other media. In fact, radio is the strongest traditional media in all multitasking studies.

Without a doubt, today (and increasingly, moving forward), the traditional media are not consumed via the usual pathways whether TV set or on paper. They have been expanding to other territories, and have gained a new life.

Radio and television programmers and newspapers will tend to expand their content delivery to other platforms and networks, to make their content available at any time, anywhere (rapidly devaluing the notion of "prime time." This will sometimes lead consumers to "stumble" on the content they and their peers produce themselves. More frequently, though, the capacity to integrate (with other media), to distribute (through multiple networks), and to diversify (content) will make the major producers (the traditional broadcasters of news and entertainment) relevant.

This evolution will be hastened as adequate measurement solutions are found. This will be the core issue of the media market, in the times ahead. Both producers and advertisers will want to know how much content is worth across the diverse platforms and networks. None of the current measurement instruments solve the key issue which the market requires knowledge on: how to measure content, across both linear distribution and interactive applications. One day, when the "lake" business (of content) imposes itself on the current "river" (of linear programming) or, when the market determines that both will coexist, complementing each other, we will find a solution.

In the last 20 years of media everything, or almost everything, has changed. Production processes have changed. Distribution has changed. The way we consume has changed.

Technological innovation will continue to surprise us and will strongly contribute to the acceleration of media convergence and content integration. In general, the technology issue is solved. We just need to see whether companies will have the capacity (and intelligence), in this hectic time of transition, to retrain people and align them with the new requirements. As always, it will be the people who will make the difference.

As Nuno Ribeiro says in his final notes, our key challenge may be the "inertia and the difficulty of adapting and reorganizing companies", equipping them with the skills required to address "the new corporate realities and challenges produced by abrupt changes".

Inertia, the inability to change our lives, can have dark consequences for us as individuals, and can be fatal to companies and governments. Thinking of this, I can't resist telling a story I once heard from Mia Couto.

Once a man saw two kids sitting on a wall.

He asked one of them: What are you doing there?

The kid answered: Nothing.

Then he asked the other one: And you, what are you doing there?

And the second kid replied: I am helping him.

We can do the same. If we want, we can see the signs – the increasing utilization of the Net; next generation mobile phones; cars equipped with IP radios, where you listen only to what you want; the growth of cable; the explosion of tablets; and the wealth of on-demand content -- as things reserved for eccentrics, and do nothing.

We can remain sitting on the wall, like the kids in Mia Couto's story, but, if we do, we will be sitting on two certainties: that this time of ours will sweep us away as easily as a tsunami, and will take along, in the flow, the wall supporting us. The walls of History also fall, as we know.

Rui Pêgo

I – Tomorrow Everything Can Change

Entering a new Era, as is the case of the new Digital Era, is not a peaceful process, whether you look at it from corporate, social, or economic viewpoints, or even at the individual level.

The impacts are huge and we will witness profound changes at all levels. Today's leaders will are unlikely to be the leaders of this new Era. We will witness the tumbling down of companies, and we will witness major changes in the behavior of individuals, with significant impacts on the consumption of goods and services.

One of the industries at the epicenter of these changes is the industry of Media and Entertainment, which will see its business models undergo changes which will forever change the production, distribution and consumption models for its products.

Change and reorganization processes are always complex and, at this moment, we are facing the challenge of understanding this new reality. In the mid-90s, the explosion of technology start-ups and unheard-of market capitalizations for these dot-coms fed the idea that these radical changes that were not possible to explain by traditional economic models and corporate management logic. Many pronounced that we were in a "New Economy".

This perception that we might be living in a new economic logic that would require new economic models was generated by the fact that we did not understand at the time that these new markets were emerging in both traditional industries (for example, digital advertising in the Media industry), and new industries such as the videogames industry.

In 2000, with many technology companies collapsing because of their lack of economic sustainability, it was clear to everyone that the laws of economics and management logic remained unchanged and valid.

Just when everything seemed to be clear, Chris Anderson, the editor-in-chief of Wired magazine, reignited the confusion with two books: The Long Tail (2006), and Free (2009).

The Long Tail is based on the theory that a product produced and distributed digitally has very low costs, allowing it to be profitable in the long term. This led to a second theory – that such abundance will ultimately lead to free products.

The changes we are currently witnessing in technology created a positive shock that has generated a productivity increase, and a decrease of distribution costs, directly impacting prices. But, as always, there is no free lunch.

Thus, Chris Anderson made some basic mistakes in his economic analysis, and ignored the capacity of management and marketing strategies to influence the behavior and consumption of consumers. He also neglected to consider the continuous emergence of new market ecosystems and new media consumption devices.

His theories have been criticized in the academic community, namely by Anita Elberse, Professor at Harvard Business School, who wrote one of the most assertive critiques.

For managers and economists the challenges are increasingly high. Everyday new realities emerge at an increasingly accelerated pace. This book intends to reflect on the challenges and realities that we live with today.

Because tomorrow everything can change.

II – Managing change in the Digital Era

Today, almost all businesses are digital. For some organizations, the digitalization of their businesses was, and still is, their major challenge from a change management viewpoint. Some have been pioneers, others have caught the "train", and others have resisted to the limit (literally). But all ended up giving in to the chip, networks, databases, data centers, electronic commerce, and online advertising.

The digitalization era opened up new horizons, but it has also changed existing paradigms in practically all industries. From the smallest companies to the biggest ones, the mandatory redesign of economic and management models has proven a decisive factor for generating positive results.

For example, Kodak had to abandon the models it had used for years to adapt to digital photography. But if for the photography industry this change is already at an advanced stage, in the Media and Entertainment industry it seems to be starting now. The Internet has unlocked the appetite for the consumption of content among the most varied audiences, expanding it the demographics of readers, spectators, users, or whatever else you want to call them.

Now, the market is the world.

Just as local media are now global, global products want to be increasingly local. Here resides the opportunity for the traditional media, since local content, local credibility and local language are definitely key differentiating factors that international players need as they seek to "translate themselves", as is, for example, the case of the Yahoo! portal and its various operations in diverse countries.

Adaptation to this new reality must be quick at this time, when new market players keep emerging with their digital DNA, dynamic management models and the seeming capacity to change constantly.

Why is it that projects like YouTube or last.fm were not created by a TV or radio station? Simply, it was because none of the traditional media had perceived the digital media as having great potential. Many have said that they "do not believe in Internet", when in reality this was not a question of faith but rather one of vision.

In many cases, inertia, lack of skills and know-how, and fear of "cannibalization" led to creative blindness regarding the utilization of these new platforms.

The media industry's change in adapting to the new paradigms is still in its beginning phases. I specifically refer to, in this context, the able management of the multiplicity of devices where content can be accessed, and understand the way content is offered to consumers. This seems simple but is rather complex.

It is precisely the "simplistic" approach that kills many efforts from the beginning.

Let us look at the Radio. In my opinion this is the medium that has the DNA closest to that of the Internet, in its power to communicate in a concise, immediate and interactive way with its audience. In radio, the telephone has always been the key channel that allowed listeners to generate content.

Radio reminds us that the UGC (User-Generated Content) concept is not new , nor was it created by the Internet, which only "baptized" it.

The major successes of the history of Radio have been programs that stimulated interactivity and the generation of contents by the listeners.

I remember that during my high school times I used to program my hi-fi set to tape record programs while i was at school. Today I subscribe to podcasts: audio, video and newsletters).

What has changed are the possibilities of technology. Today we can permanently access contents via computer, mobile phone, Playstation, iPhone, iPod, iPad, and Kindle, among many other devices.

The media distribution sector also suffers the same "cannibalization" fear, continuing to feed the format "war" – DVD, HD DVD and BluRay – even when it is all too clear that downloads and real-time streaming on-demand will prevail.

Apple clearly understood this trend and ignored all the criticisms of its AppleTV set-top box regarding its lack of a DVD reader, as it had long since positioned itself in the digital distribution market with iTunes.

In this new globalization and digitalization reality, no matter what industry you look at, I believe that the winners will be those players that have the strongest capacity to adapt and quickly implement new ways of management. Darwin[1] made a similar statement, in a different context: the more capable will survive – and they are not always the strongest, but are always the more adaptive.

And if this sea change in organizations is important to consider, it is also relevant for consideration of the world's nations, which are increasingly dependent on the digitalization of their industries, and even more so now, in these times of crisis psychoses, where human survival is indeed a real and practical issue.

III – Visionaries

At the beginning of Internet era many forecasts were made about the impact it would have on society. As these forecasts became reality, various names emerged to describe what was happening and being forecasted, e.g., "revolution of communications", "information highway", "revolution of information" and "digital revolution" to name a few. What only a few understood is that we had entered a whole new era, the Digital Era.

Nicholas Negroponte, founder of the Media Lab at Massachusetts Institute of Technology (MIT), one of the first and probably the most respected of visionaries, shared his ideas in the book Being Digital[2]. Negroponte explains the basis underlying the change toward the Digital Era: the transformation of atoms into bits. That is, he discussed the transition of many businesses from physical to digital, and the impact it will have on the various industries.

The founder of Microsoft, Bill Gates, was another visionary booster of this new Era, as expressed in his The Path to the Future[3].

Despite what it said in the books published, it soon became clear that the new technologies would generate major socioeconomic change. The exuberant visions and forecasts created expectations about the short-term results caused what is known as "Internet bubble".

The key reasons for the delay in the materialization of these original visions and forecasts have been the following:

- The maturating and democratization of technology and access to the broadband Internet was slower than expected.

- The diverse industries that saw their core businesses threatened resisted change, avoiding and delaying shifts in their business models and operations, which created opportunities for the new players in various industries – Music, Media, Retail, travel and others.

Today no one has doubts regarding the impact of "bits" in society. We have entered the Digital Era and as we move forward in it the pace of change is even quicker. Many industries and professions will change radically or even disappear, and new business opportunities, new markets and new professional skills will emerge.

For example, the media have new content distribution channels which create opportunities to reach new markets more easily, with new (on-line) advertising formats for advertisers and new business models for the sale of content and/or services. These new channels require the development of new skills including the analysis and measurement of audiences (traffic analyst and manager), how to program campaigns in new tools (advertising operations), and more.

The Digital Era requires ever more rationality in the management of organizations, where technology plays an increasingly important role in management efficiency.

It is already evident that organizations have to reinvent themselves, that businesses have to be more innovative, and that new management and political leaders will emerge. Existential questions on whether the new model is capitalist or socialist also emerge[4].

IV – Changes to the Media Business Model

Digitalization and network communication through IP (Internet Protocol) are the engines of in-depth change to almost everything we witness in today's society. All industries have seen their business and operations models transformed -- but the one that has felt the greatest impact was Media & Entertainment...and we are just feeling the first tremor of a major earthquake...

This "new world" for the media & entertainment industry opens up new opportunities but requires a major new understanding the ensuring social and economic changes. Some of these changes and impacts were anticipated in 1998 by the cyber-futurologist Chuck Martin in his book Net Future[5].

In this industry, the major seismic events have been and are being caused by the following three factors:
- Content convergence
- Web 2.0 (social networks)
- The generational factor – the crossing of four generations: Baby Boomers, Generation X, Generation X, and the Digital Natives.

IV.1 - Content Convergence

The largest paradigm shift in the media industry has been the convergence of contents – this has had deep impact on the whole operation of the media.

- Production of digital content
For the media, the impact on production techniques was huge. For the first time, textual, audio, image and video content share the same platforms, enriching information and entertainment with multimedia content.

- Distribution changes and is more competitive

Media distribution platforms, even the traditional ones, are shifting to digital technology (for example, DVB – Digital Video Broadcasting, and DAB -Digital Audio Broadcast). The same content is available on multiple devices[6], many of them evolved and converged, feature-wise.

As the content offerings have increased significantly, the borders amongst distribution media have vanished. The traditional content splits are absent in the digital media, where the "press", radio and TV industries are competing in the same space for audiences and revenues. In addition, digital platforms based on IP distribution have low entry barriers, which has led to the increase in new market entries.

- Fragmentation of audiences

The various possibilities offered to consumers for accessing content has caused the fragmentation of audiences onto multiple platforms and devices, which has led to a major change of the consumption model and paradigm that Christian Nissen called "The Lake"[7], where consumers choose what they want at the time they want and on the device they want. Thus they end the "dictatorship of programming" and linear consumption.

- Sources of revenue

Traditional advertising has for long been the only source of revenue for broadcast TV and Radio. In the case of the printed press, newsstand sales and advertising were the two key sources of revenues. Today, the reality for all of these media is different as they are scattered along several platforms creating new digital advertising markets (including display, search, branded content, branded experience, branded engagement, in-game advertising, rich media, etc.).

The business has become more complex and requires deep changes in the media organizations, mainly at the technology and HR levels.

The digital platforms have enabled the ability to measure audiences in real time, which also represents a major change in the ways of managing and creating advertising offerings.

Furthermore, digital media has also created the possibility for new business models to emerge, namely paid content (e.g., cable TV channels,

DVB, sale of content on-line, etc.), the sale of physical and digital goods, and other services on these new platforms.

- New costs

The changes to the digital business model have implied that organizations should have HR structures with new qualifications and job profiles. Despite the fact that, in some situations, the distribution and production costs of digital media are lower, and that they benefit from the synergies in content production among digital and traditional platforms, the production and distribution of digital contents requires some caution. Unlike traditional broadcast distribution, that does not require additional costs to provide content to an additional consumer, digital distribution has offered increasingly low costs, due to ongoing technology innovation (Moore's Law). But, there are costs associated with each additional consumer – bandwidth, disk space, server processing and electric power, unlike what Chris Anderson (the editor in chief of Wired magazine) tries to convey in his book – Free[8]. The theories he describes in his books The Long Tail[9] and Free have serious faults from an economic viewpoint. These faults are caused by concept confusion. "Social movements" of collaboration and sharing are confused with "free", not understanding the real costs for digital hosting and distribution, and by not incorporating the influence of marketing and communication costs in the sale of goods and services (physical and digital).

For example, YouTube has a critical and complex problem to manage: the fact that only 4% of the content hosted generates significant traffic and revenue potential. But, according to the business model created by YouTube (and used by other social networks), it has to host and serve all the videos that users publish.

Thus, it has excess hosting and maintenance costs for content not seen, which also refutes Chris Anderson's theory in The Long Tail, since even if there are advertising revenues associated with these videos, hosting and provision costs throughout the years will never be paid by advertising.

The old economic saying still goes "There are no free lunches."

- Cloud Computing:

From the organization's viewpoint, there is today a strong trend to have data centers "outdoors" and to focus on business, while minimizing technology cost. The resistances to cloud computing regarding security, confidentiality and reliability will disappear with time, and the productivity gains will be a strong argument[10] for adoption.

For individuals, the ability to access applications – work, communication and entertainment tools – and professional or personal documents using different devices (computer, mobile phone, tablet, etc.) will become a vital and natural service.

Regarding the devices themselves, cloud computing will also cause significant changes, as they will require less processing and storage capacity – performed in the "cloud" – and they will become more "basic" and cheaper devices.

IV.2 – Web 2.0 (Social networks)

Web 2.0 has managed to demonstrate its potential through the social networks. The sustained growth of the Facebook audience proves that.

The changes in devices allow not only the ability to access content but also the ability to create, publish and share it, either via computer, netbook, tablet or mobile phone.

In the next years, new social networks will emerge segmented by topics and groups, within the "general" social networks, recovering the web 1.0 concept of "Virtual Communities" built around contents, behaviors, celebrities, etc. A good example is the social network created around the candidate, and now president of the USA, Barack Obama – My.BarackObama.com.

This is a clear sign of the times, and of the importance of social networks in conveying the information and fostering the gathering of people around a topic, a cause, a personality and a candidate.

IV.3 – Generational Factor

Four generations (Baby Boomers, Generation X, Generation Y, and Generation Z) changed the way of working, communicating, and having relationships.

Digital Natives **+**

Generation Z (Born after 1996t)
Cannot imagine their lives without internet, mobile phones or consoles. These are part of their DNA.

Generation Y (Born between 1980 and 1995)
This is the largest population in the digital media. Internet is part of their lives as they are the first digital natives, they followed its evolution.

Generation X (Born between 1965 and 1979)
The majority uses internet mainly at work but are not dependant.

Baby Boomers (Born between 1946 and 1964)
Only a small percentage of this generation migrated to internet and rarely for entertainment purposes. Internet is usually used as a second media for information research. This group has been increasing both in number and permanence in the digital media since they have greater time availability.

Digital Emigrants **-**

Veterans (Born between 1925 and 1945)
These are almost residual in the digital media. They have a limited utilization of the media and highly focused.

The Baby Boomers, who had greater difficulties adapting to the new technologies, are today strong "allies" of Generation Y (their children or grandchildren)[11].

Digital platforms have built bridges among generations. Today, it is easy and natural for grandparents, parents and grandchildren to communicate via email, Skype, instant messenger, FaceTime and even social networks.

Beyond the higher ease of communication, there is a higher frequency of frequency and better sharing of interests and information.

The Internet has brought all generations closer as it fosters communication and opinion sharing in real time.

In the United States, the country where the digital culture is most developed, the Baby Boomer generation, which is still professionally active and playing important roles in big organizations, has brought in young recent graduates as their advisors, to help them think and redesign their businesses incorporating the digital variable[11].

The adaptation of older generations to new technologies and their adherence to the Internet has been increasing due to mass market broadband and the better usability of devices, applications and sites.

V – On-line Advertising

On-line advertising officially started on October 27, 1994 on the HotWired site (now wired.com). This was the date the first on-line advertising campaign ran, and the first on-line advertiser was the American telecom operator AT&T, with a twelve-week campaign.

The traditional 468x60 pixel banner was created by the interactive agency Modem Media (now part of the Publicis Group). The contract was worth $33,000 to HotWired[12].

The following year, Yahoo! changed its portal's design in order to accommodate advertising.

The first on-line advertisers were mainly telecom and technology companies, and the first users were technology geeks, which made the sites an excellent way of communicating with target consumers.

This was also one of the reasons why technology review sites, such as CNET and ZDNet, became the early audience leaders and defined new advertising patterns. As the screen resolution increased, CNET created new ad sizes that became standards, such as the leaderboard, skyscraper and "mrec" (medium rectangle.)

Not only have ad sizes changed, but technologies now allow increasingly richer forms of creativity (using video, flash, javascript, etc.). Add to this the possibilities of optimization tools applied to on-line advertising management, and you can ensure a level of effectiveness none of the traditional media can offer.

Beyond segmentation by region, day, hour, frequency, and type of content, it is also possible to create behavioral segments (behavioral targeting) where advertising is displayed according to the history of content consumed by users, for example: economy, sports, technology, etc.

Interactive video advertising on the digital platforms is the format having the highest potential, which is being stimulated by sites with video contents, such as YouTube, and videocasts, where video advertising is clearly the most effective format.

Advertising on sites and applications optimized for mobile devices will also be an area experiencing stronger growth in coming years, stimulated by increasing mobile bandwidth (4G and Wi-Fi) and by the new features and strengths of these equipments (e.g., iPhone and iPad).

And finally, advertising in videogames is possibly the most innovative area of digital advertising since is gives the possibility of a campaign that can cross multiple formats (banners, videos and in-game advertising), linked to the growing number of videogame users and to its strengths, advertising in scenarios that simulate realities, e.g., soccer arenas.

The complexity and range of on-line communication formats adds, for creative and media agencies, higher complexity in the definition of communication strategies and how to interact with consumers.

Investments in digital platforms will keep growing in a sustained way, given the natural shift in audiences and also due to the convergence of media to the digital platforms.

VI – Videogames

The evolution of information technologies has not only allowed a broader access to information and communication, on multiple platforms, but also to entertainment. Videogames have left the arcades and game rooms to enter users' households and pockets (on portable consoles and mobile phones).

The videogames industry has been showing one of the highest growth rates in the area of media and entertainment). It also presents greater growth potential for the next years.

To understand this growth trend it is important to analyze the following:
- The videogames market
- The sources of revenues
- The audience / profile of gamers
- Advertising in videogames

VI.1 - The Videogames Market

In the Global Entertainment and Media Outlook 2009-¬2013 market research conducted by PricewaterhouseCoopers[13], the estimate for revenues generated by the videogames industry amounted to 51.4 billion dollars in 2008, with expected growth to 73.5 billion dollars in 2013. Should there be an error in these estimates, it can only be on the low end since recent news points towards increasingly accelerated growth, expected to be much higher than the conservative 6.9% annual average growth indicated in the PricewaterhouseCoopers study).

In 2008, in Portugal, over 2.5 million videogames were sold[14] ,beating for the first time the unit sales of movies in DVD format. In the USA, the number of games sold was more than 268 million units[15] for the three console platforms (Nintendo, Sony and Microsoft) alone.

Forecasts for 2009 and 2010 continue to point towards growth in all markets[14] (the ones analyzed include: North America, EMEA, Asia-Pacific, and Latin America).

One proof of this growth was the successive news, in 2009, of increasing sales records. In May 2009, the action game Grand Theft Auto IV sold over 6 million copies in only one week, with revenues above 500 million dollars (including 3.6 million copies and 310 million dollars on the first day of sales)[16].

Then, in the month of November, Activision, published Call Of Duty: Modern Warfare 2 (a war simulator), and announced the sale of 4.7 million copies on the first day in North America and the UK. This generated over 310 million dollars, and then 13 million units sold in the first month in these two markets alone, beating the results of Grand Theft Auto IV[14 and 17]. These figures are way higher than those of the box office receipts of most of Hollywood's major productions.

The social network phenomenon is another one of the videogame industry's drivers. The publishers Zynga and Playfish distribute and promote many of their games and have exponentially increased the popularity and use of their titles. This popularity attracted the attention of investors, resulting in Playfish being acquired in November 2009 by one of the major world publishers of videogames[18] EA (Electronic Arts[19] which paid over 400 million dollars for the company.

Zynga itself has been valued ag over a billion dollars, and the Russian venture capital company Digital Sky Technologies invested 180 million dollars in Zynga in December 2009[20].

Google has still not revealed its plans for this industry but has already given signs that it is paying attention and preparing its moves[21], including registering a patent for the Web-Based System for Generation of Interactive Games Based on Digital Videos.

VI.2 - The Sources of Revenues

Initially, the sources of revenues from videogames were the coins required to play on the consoles installed at arcades and game rooms. The business and profitability variables depended on factors such as the distribution and location of consoles, which were not controlled nor managed by publishers.

The evolution of technology allows us today to have consoles and other devices at home, or in our pockets (mobile phones and portable consoles).

This radical change in distribution, and the mass market adoption of videogames has allowed publishers to create games with revenue models, beyond the unit sales of titles.

And games that are MMOGs (massively multiplayer online games) have at least five different revenue streams: sale, subscription, extra content, sale of digital goods and in-game advertising.

- Sale

Selling videogames does not depend on physical distribution anymore, and the business is steadily increasing in digital on-line shops (e.g., Steam, Metaboli, GameTap, etc.) and in the "App Stores" of the console and mobile device manufacturers (on-line shops selling applications, such as Playstation Store, Wii Shop, iTunes-App Store, Xbox Live Market Place, OVI, etc.).

- Subscription of services

Many MMOGs require or at least offer subscription services. World of Warcraft, for example, requires a subscription fee of 10 euros per month, and counts over 12 million loyal players, a number that earned it an entry in the Guinness Book of World Records" [22 and 23].

Another example is the on-line soccer games by PowerChallenge (PowerSoccer, and ManagerZone), where players can optionally subscribe to "club membership", and receive additional functionalities.

- Extra content (downloadable content)

Some games offer the possibility of buying additional content for a videogame, such as Singstar (a karaoke videogame), where it is possible to acquire music on-line to add to the game.

- Digital goods

In MMOGs, digital goods allow users to stand out, showing off their personalities or those of their avatars. The sale of digital goods is thus a very interesting source of revenues for publishers. In the case of the online games from PowerChallenge, users can acquire the following for their soccer teams: boots, tattoos, distinctive ways of celebrating goals, haircuts, beards, "charismatic" coaches, and more.

- In-game advertising

The broad audiences that videogames can reach today, plus a built-in thematic affinity many games have with some audiences, has awakened the interest of brands/advertisers in communicating within the game environment. Such advertisements also convey greater realism and deep involvement with the players (see Chapter VI.4 – Advertising in Videogames).

VI.3 - The audience/profile of gamers

Videogames are reaching more and more audiences, and playing them is no longer solely an individual activity -- it has turned into a collective one both due to the capability of playing on the network and because consoles are leaving the bedrooms of young people and being installed in living rooms, thus becoming a family entertainment activity.

Player behavior has also changed. MMOGs have transformed users from simple consumers to active contributors to the game content as they "personalize" the environment of the game, that is then shared with other users.

The current profile of players[24, 25 and 26] is primarily masculine (60%), and 48% are active players (playing over 8 hours a week). Among women this indicator falls to 29%. These players have an average age of 36, and are students or have higher education degrees (50%). Their income is above average, and they are intense consumers of new technologies and gadgets, making them strong influencers of technology purchases. They connect to the Internet around five times per day and play online (60%).

VI.4 - Advertising in Videogames

Advertising in videogames is still a novelty but the results are proven in various studies[24, 25, 27 and 28]. The level of attention to the action of the game is high, so the advertising does not go unnoticed, and is even appreciated by players, since it makes the game environment more real.

For example, the results of a zappos.com in-game campaign[28] in 2009 registers an effectiveness rate 500% higher than a TV campaign:
 - Players who watched the campaign remembered a brand five times more than those who did not.
 - There was a 56% increase of positive perception about the brand/company.
 - Players who watched the campaign had a high recall rate during the game (TV can only reach a medium level).

There are four main ways of using videogames to communicate ad messages:
 - **Static integration** are the inclusion of brands directly in the game's storyline, integrating the products as elements of the game, whether they be a car, a soccer ball, boots or anything else. someone having bought the sponsor's product can receive a digital good or extra credits in the game for free.
 - **Videogames tailored for a brand or product (advergames),** often to promote specific models of a car brand; these games can be distributed on CD Rom and/or on the brand's site.
 - **Co-marketing actions,** involving promotions at the point of sale oriented toward the users of a specific videogame, so that the player can get a special discount and/or
 - **Dynamic in-game advertising** is distributed in a dynamic way within the videogame environment with a programming and distribution model equivalent to Internet campaigns (a number of impressions is set to be distributed at planned time slots). These impressions are measured by time - for every 10 cumulative seconds of exposure an impression is counted (and counting only starts if the individual exposures are greater than half a second).

VII – People and Leaders

We know that human resources are the essence of any business. When Jack Welch, considered by many to be the best CEO of all time, came to Lisbon in 2006 to participate in the Forum for Competitiveness Conference, he stressed the importance of the human factor in management, as well as the need to look for talent, to train it and to develop it. He treated the director of human resources as his right-hand man, and revealed that the secret of success in any company is to keep employees excited, customers satisfied, and to guarantee results for shareholders. The formula even seems "simple" and effective!

Why is it that most companies cannot implement it?
Because it is not as simple as it looks. To make this "magic potion," many ingredients and special seasonings are required for each case.

In the digital media industry, human resources are an even larger differentiating factor since there is the need to understand something that is new. And this is only possible with people that have a strong understanding of technology and media, how they have evolved in time, and have a high amount of digital culture in their DNA.

Jerry Yang, the co-founder of Yahoo! wrote in 2000[29]: "Without responsible actions, this media (the Internet) can disappear as quickly as it emerged. The future of the Net depends on the people as much as it depends on technology".

Ten years on, the debate is not about the survival of Internet anymore but rather the survival of some projects vs. others. And the truth is that if we analyze the more successful companies in digital media,
the human factor clearly stands out.

The leaders of these companies have understood the potential of

Internet as a medium, and always keep in their "mental algorithm" the specific logics of digital businesses.

Steve Jobs, CEO of Apple, is the most notable proof of this. Regardless of criticism or praise, he has had the "digital factor" fully incorporated in his DNA since the first "chips". Jobs understands media as well as advertising (he was able to invent and reinvent the Apple brand turning it into a loved brand) and made us think different (which became an attitude and not just a slogan).

That Steve Jobs also has knowledge across multiple sectors: technology (hardware and software), the movies industry (Pixar), Internet and the media (Disney) is today evident in Apple strategy.

Some people say that Steve Jobs represents 20% of Apple value. Such a view is given credibility when we consider the impact of a rumor on October 3, 2008: Apple stock fell 10% after the news that Jobs had had a stroke, and immediately recovered after the official denial by Apple.

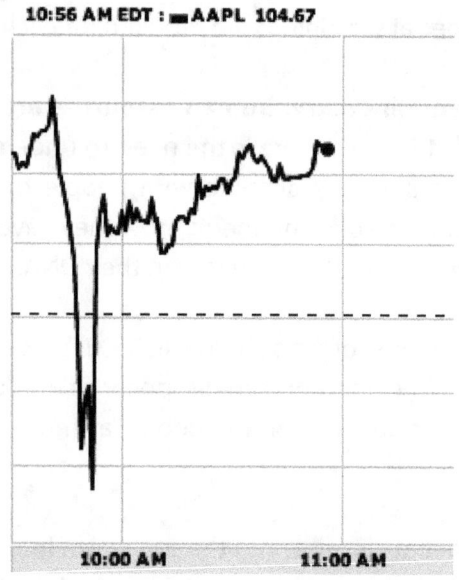

Evolution of Apple stocks in the morning of October 3, 2008

The ups and downs, the eternal question marks placed on the future and the value of people in the companies are nothing more than signs of change of our society. Not all generations have had the privilege of living change. We do!

Until this day, the one change that caused a greater impact was the discovery of electricity and the changes that it brought, and the impact it had on people's lives, on companies and on society. As for the role of people, were it not for Edison's singular talent, who knows if we would not still be in the dark today?

VIII- Politics

Improving the effectiveness and the results of companies in this time of uncertainty we live in is the topic of the book Leadership In The Era Of Economic Uncertainty[30] by Ram Charan, considered one of the current gurus of management. Charan suggests that the "innovation factor" is one of the key factors in leadership.

At a conference at the Portuguese Catholic University in Lisbon in March 2009, David Plouffe, director of Barack Obama's campaign, referred to the factors that led to the election of the current president of the United States. Communications innovation via social networks was one of the differentiating factors of their electoral communication strategy.

The new management models referred by Ram Charan have a practical case as applied to politics, as David Plouffe presented.

As a coincidence, or maybe not, Fast Company magazine published an article in March 2009[31] highlighting the 50 most innovative companies, and first place was granted to the "Obama Team". The team was considered as a start-up, having started its activity in February 2007, when Obama announced he was running for the presidency, and launched the MyBO social network – MyBarackObama.com. Since its launch, over 2 million users and 35 thousand volunteer groups have registered, and 200 thousand events were organized and promoted. The "Obama Team" bet on technology to communicate with voters given its high speed and effectiveness at low costs.

Plouffe notes that the Internet served to create "foundational organizations", allowed citizens to get closer to politics, and closer to a project that reflected the expectations of many and to which many contributed with work and money (with almost 1 billion dollars donated). Despite the fact that many have said that it was the Internet that elected Barack Obama, Plouffe prefers to say that the election of the new president was only possible because "it was possible to convey a consistent message". Actually, the Internet was the media chosen from the very beginning, for its huge power and for the fact that it encouraged a network communication effect (with each user sharing with his/her friends and colleagues). This was the viral/social effect that the "Obama Team" wanted to achieve, and they knew how to get across this "consistent message," how to face competitors, clarify their positions to voters, and receive feedback on what was going on in the field.

Management in companies and in politics is but the same. If we could have Ram Charan and David Plouffe around a table, I am sure that they would have many points in common, as it is being increasingly proven that innovation in life, in politics or in companies plus a consistent message creates positive results.

IX – Concentration and Pluralism

If there is an industry where the discussion on market share concentration and regulation has never been peaceful, it is the media and entertainment industry.

With the convergence of content generated by the possibility of digital distribution[7] it seemed evident that the natural development of business would lead to the "marriage" of media and telecom companies. And, in fact, this happened in several countries.

The most notable and largest example was that of the merger of Time Warner and AOL in January 2000. But, when the dot-com "bubble" burst[32] this initial combination trend cooled off.

The fragmentation of audiences and the consequent change in the distribution of advertising investment, caused by the new (digital) options, as well as the shifts in media consumption paradigms are forcing new M&A moves by media companies. Legislation has also failed to adapt to the needs imposed by the market changes and paradigm shifts[7]. The low barriers to entry (for digital platforms) for a media company and the need for research and innovation have become important business variables.

The paradigm shifts will also cause industry concentration that will allow higher competitiveness (among major groups), and the capacity to invest in innovation, to adapt to technological trends and develop new products. One of the most recent examples of concentration was the acquisition of the NBC television network by the telecom/cable operator Comcast[33], in December 2009.

Concentration moves can ensure higher competitiveness as the result is media groups with stronger investment capacity and greater abilities to realize synergies. It is thus natural that regulators should become more liberal and let Adam Smith's "Invisible Hand"[34] make the natural market adjustments.

Diagonal concentration

Legislators and regulators have been focusing on preventing excessive power in specific markets, and have been reviewing and creating legislation for vertical and horizontal concentration, ignoring the interdependencies that exist with other industries/markets.

In the new Digital Era, interdependency among industries can be decisive for the success of an operator since a dominant position in one market can leverage a position in another market, which makes it difficult to analyze a company's individual market power isolated from other variables. For example, the theory of the hypothetical monopolist hardly applies in the analysis of this type of concentration.

Thus, legislators and regulators have new challenges and new econometric analyses to perform on market interdependency.

Pluralism

Throughout time there have always been control of the media and attempts to control and manipulate them by political, religious and business groups.

The changes caused by the Digital Era put us before new realities such as the concept of the citizen reporter, blogs, microblogging, social networks and the possibility for consumer to comment and interact with media content. This guarantees that today it is impossible to control information. In the digital platforms we will have all the possible opinion streams present, sharing of information and the respective reactions.

Nicholas Negroponte referred in 1995 in his visionary prophecies on the digital revolution that "the combination of technological forces and human nature will play a stronger role in pluralism than any other law issued by the Congress"[2].

The adjustment and initial impact on this new reality was also anticipated by Negroponte:

"There is pure and simply no way of limiting the freedom of bit radiation, just like the Romans could not stop the spread of Christianity, even if during the process some of the first and brave diffusers of data are eaten by Washington lions"[2].

The Wikileaks phenomenon, whether we agree or disagree with its way of acting, has been generating news worldwide and is a good example of what Negroponte forecast. This unlimited freedom is doubtless the most significant guarantee of pluralism in the history of humanity.

X – World Giants

Today, the key world players leading the creation and definition of future paths in the Digital Era are Apple, Google, Microsoft, Nokia, Sony, and Amazon.com.

All of them have created incompatible ecosystems[35], and are trying to capture the major share in various markets and sub-markets where they are present, and are betting strongly in leveraging their positions among thevarious markets. Thus, the diversification of businesses is vital to capture dominant positions but also strongly increases management complexity.

Strategic and operational management in each of the sub-markets where they are present is a decisive factor in ensuring success. They pursue what Warren Buffet has called the "Consumer Monopoly" and the "Toll Bridge"[36]. They know that the winner takes it all and therefore will not spare efforts, time or investments because there can be no "prize" for the number two – knowing, however, that there may be some markets where there can be some strong competitors.

In this "race," the symbiosis between (on-line) devices and services can be a decisive factor against competitors, closing down the chances for them to reach captured customers. Consumers are now starting to have "exit barriers", and the integration of services among the various brand devices ensures higher fidelity levels and lower price elasticity on the demand side.

Therefore, the goal now is to capture higher share in each of the markets and to create leverage effects among them. Wild competition, how continuous technological evolution creates the possibility of new entrants, and the quick changes in media consumption habits are important variables to be considered by any of the aforementioned titans. I will now briefly analyze the presence of each one of the companies in the markets (and sub-markets) of Hardware/Devices, Software, Web and on-line Distribution.

Devices/Hardware

	Apple	Google	Microsoft	Nokia	Sony	Amazon
PC	Mac			Booklet	Various	
SmarthPhone	iPhone	NexusOne *	KIN **	Various	Various	
MP3 reader	iPod, iPhone, iPad		Zune	Various Mobiles	Walkman, Various Mobiles	
Games Console	iPod Touch, iPhone, iPad		XBox	Various Mobiles	Playstation, PSP	
TV					Various	
Set-Top Box	Apple TV	Google TV ***	XBox MediaRoom ****			
Tablet	iPad	Google Tablet *****			Reader	Kindle

* Google discontinued NexusOne mobile phone in July 2010 (seven months after launch).

** KIN was launched on May 13, 2010, and was discontinued on June 30, 2010.

*** Google is preparing a set-top box and software – Google TV – that can be offered on TV sets. Sony will be one of the manufacturers to include Google's operating system and respective applications on TV sets.

**** MediaRoom is the sofware Microsoft offers to cable operators and Internet Service Providers (for the provision of IPTV services) for set-top boxes and also for Xbox (e.g., Vodafone Home TV).

***** Google has already announced the launch of Google Tablet but not a date. The equipment will be manufactured by HTC (as in the case of Nexus One mobile phone).

Software

	Apple	Google	Microsoft	Nokia	Sony	Amazon
Computer Operational System	MacOS	Android	Windows			
Mobile Operational System	iOS	Android Mobile	Windows Phone	Symbian*		
Browser	Safari	Chrome	Internet Explorer			
Productivity	iWork, iLife, and others	GoogleDocs (web)	Office, and others			
B2B solutions	HW/SW for various industries	GoogleApps	SW for various industries	HW/SW for mobiles	HW/SW for the broadcast industry	Amazon Web Services

* Nokia has sold the Symbian operating system in July 2009 to Accenture.

Web

	Apple	Google	Microsoft	Nokia	Sony	Amazon
Portal (contents)	lala * (music)	YouTube (UCG video)	MSN			
Search Engine		Google	Bing			A9
Ad Server Display		DoubleClick	Atlas			
Ad Server Search		AdSense, AdWords	Bing			ClickRive
Ad Server Mobile	iAd	DoubleClick, AdMob	ScreenTonic			
Ad Server In-Game		AdScapeMedia	Massive **			
Webmail	Mobile.Me	GMail	Hotmail, Live	OviMail		
Messenger		GTalk	Messenger			
Maps	PlaceBase Poly9	GoogleMaps	Bing Maps	OviMaps		
Others		Various	Various		PlayStation Home	Alexa

* Apple has discontinued its music streaming portal on May 31, 2010. It is likely that the lala platform will be integrated in iTunes, allowing for streaming service.

** Microsoft discontinued its Massive division and in-game advertising platform in October 2010.

On-line Distribution

	Apple	Google	Microsoft	Nokia	Sony	Amazon
On-line Shops	iTunes	Android Market	Zune Marketplace XBox Marketplace Windows Phone Marketplace	Ovi Store	PlayStation Store eBookStore PlayNow Arena	Amazon.com

On each one of the titans:

Apple

Its strong brand is associated with innovation, design, lifestyle and fashion, and the excellent usability of its hardware and software ensure a high fidelity level. Apple built a "consumer monopoly" and on May 26, 2010 overtook Microsoft in market capitalization, now being the major technology company[37], and the second worldwide (after the oil company Exxon Mobil). If analysts' projections of Apple results and market shares are correct, it could soon be the most valuable company in the world.

The fact that it produces hardware and develops software gives Apple a huge competitive advantage vis-à-vis its key competitors. iPad sales have been highly successful - it is the mobile device with the fastest adoption rate, reaching a record of three million units sold in eighty days only[38].

Sales of the new iPhone 4 also reached an impressive 1.7 million units in the first three days, and three million in the first three weeks[39], beating the iPad.

iTunes is the core platform for content distribution ("toll bridge"), announcing in February 2010[40] that it hit the record of 10 billion tunes sold, making it the biggest store of digital goods (music, games, books and applications).

Apple reacted to Google's entry into advertising management platforms on mobile platforms, and acquired Quattro Wireless[41] in January 2010. Leveraging this platform, they created iAd[42], an advertising service.

But if their goal is to broadly enter into advertising management platforms (search, display, and in-game) it will have to be quick in development and/or acquisition.

In the TV market Apple has the set-top box Apple TV. In February 2010, Steve Jobs referred in the Wall Street Journal conference D8[43] that it was about a hobby (since the sales were poor), but Tim Cook, COO of Apple, some days afterwards, at the Goldman Sachs conference on technology, said that, "We feel that there is something in the TV market... we may present something in this area"[44]. In September 2010, a new version of Apple TV was launched, which proves that Apple still wants to have a position in this area.

Google

The popular search engine has attained impressive market share. The brand (a "Consumer Monopoly") ranked first in 2009 in BrandZ ranking with a valuation of 100 billion dollars[45].

Google directly declared "war" on Microsoft with the operating systems Android and Android Mobile, the Chrome browser and Google Docs (web-based productivity applications).

The big cash cow is still the AdWords advertising platform (a "toll bridge"). Google is the leader in advertising management platforms and is present in all sub-segments: Search (AdWords), Display (DoubleClick), Mobile (DoubleClick and AdMob), and In-Game (adScape Media).

Their entry in mobile devices (in partnership with HTC) is still far from being a success, and the partnership with Apple (with the integration of Google services in Apple devices) is at "risk" based on the fact that it entered the mobile phone market and is in the process of preparing devices to compete with iPad and Apple TV.

Google has already announced that it is preparing the launch of Google Tablet[46] (also to be manufactured by HTC) and that will also enter the market of set-top boxes with GoogleTV through partnerships with Intel and Sony[47] (Google software will be offered on TV sets of the Japanese manufacturer).

It can be expected that Google will once more enter the value chain of advertising; Google AdWords already allows advertising on some TV stations but, if Google software allows footer advertising, for example, (regardless of the channel, and to be programmed according to the audience's profile), will there be revenue sharing with TV operators?

To what extent and how will regulators intervene? As I mentioned in the previous chapter, new challenges will emerge also for regulators.

Microsoft

Microsoft's approach is highly focused on software and on reaching massive market share for the Windows operating system via almost all hardware manufacturers, thus granting Microsoft a strong advantage in the distribution of its operating system and other applications.

The mobile phone of Microsoft, the KIN (manufactured by Sharp), might have been the mobile phone with the shortest life -- it was launched on May 13, 2010 and discontinued on June 30, 2010.

Microsoft's Xbox also grants Internet Service Providers the possibility of offering TV services with Xbox / Media Room[50], as is the case in Portugal with the Vodafone Home TV service.

The ease of integration among Microsoft applications, either for domestic or corporate users, grants them also a competitive advantage for the creation of a "Consumer Monopoly" and "Toll Bridge".

The "war" with Apple in MP3 players was fought with Zune; the war with Sony and Nintendo in games consoles is fought with Xbox. Nevertheless, the software giant took a long time to understand the steps it had to take on Internet, and it took a lot of time to materialize.

In the Web market, Microsoft is present in all segments, and also partners with Yahoo! for the integration of its search engine Bing. This sale of advertising could be the smooth preparation for a successful takeover bid, after the failed one in 2008. But there are currently other companies interested. In April 2010, Nokia and Yahoo! established a strategic partnership that could indicate the possibility of another type of relationship in the future[51].

The creation of the Bing search engine and the acquisition of the AdServer Atlas (after an attempt to acquire DoubleClick), positioned

Microsoft as direct competitor of Google, but with significantly lower market share.

Nokia

Nokia is the only European company in this fight of titans. With high credibility and name recognition, Nokia is also known for its continuous change culture. But it has been asleep with its large market share ("Consumer Monopoly"), and has taken too long to react to touchscreens, having been beaten by HTC and Apple, and has thus lost its advantage in the smartphone segment.

However, it is still the mobile device manufacturer with the largest global market share (approximately 40%). Today it is preparing to become a media company[52] focusing its activity on the integration of services and contents.

The sale of its mobile operating system Symbian to Accenture[53], and the utilization of other operating systems in its equipment – such as the open-source system Maemo in the Nokia N900 – as well as the announcement of a partnership with Microsoft show a change of strategy in this area. Ovi Store will be an important lever of this change of strategy, where the number of Nokia devices will be an important revenue driver for the Ovi Store ("Toll Bridge").

Their recent attempt to enter the notebook market with the Booklet laptop was a shy and late one that produced poor results. There is still no news about a Nokia tablet but, should it happen, it might be too late.

Their recent strategic partnership with Yahoo! consists of[51] providing maps and navigation services to Yahoo!, and the utilization of Yahoo! email and chat platforms for Nokia customers.

With this strategic alliance the questions that rise are the following:
- Will this be the beginning of a "courtship" that could end in a takeover bid or merger?
- Will the alliance of Yahoo! with Microsoft continue?

Sony

The Japanese giant's strategy is based on hardware devices and on-line shops, and its brand awareness and the reliability of its products are two of its strengths ("Consumer Monopoly").

Televisions are an important device given the possibilities of Internet connectivity and access to on-line services, where its partnership with Google[47] to offer its operating system could be a sales driver.

The Playstation 3 console can also position itself as a media center. As to PlayStation Portable Go, it is expected to evolve toward PlayStation Phone, a console and mobile phone, which could also be a major lever of the on-line services and sales (Playstation Store = "Toll Bridge").

The eReader by Sony is still far from the features of the market leader, iPad, and has a residual market share[54]. It is thus natural that Sony will relaunch a new eReader or discontinue it.

Amazon.com

Amazon.com is the reference brand for electronic commerce ("Consumer Monopoly" and "Toll Bridge"), a position gained via the ongoing evolution of its CRM system and its high level of customer service.

The perception that books (its initial sales focus) would evolve toward digital formats led to the production of the eReader Kindle, expanding the market for the sale of books in digital formats as well as music with Amazon MP3.

The growth of Amazon implied major infrastructure investments and today it provides cloud computing services – Amazon Web Services – an important trend for the next years where it is already well positioned ("Toll Bridge").

Amazon owns the Alexa.com site that analyzes on-line audience statistics and trends (by segment, country, etc.). It also owns the A9.com search engine that is integrated with the ClickRiver advertising platform.

These titans will mark the next years but, like in other industries, not always the most powerful survive, as Professor Jim Collins cautions in his book How the Mighty Fall and Why Some Companies Never Give In[55].

XI – Final Notes

The Digital Era will fully change the history of humanity, and will be the most significant change we will witness after the Industrial Revolution.

As strange as it may seem, this being an Era where technology will strongly predominate, organizations and countries will be even more dependent on the talent and knowledge of their employees and leaders than in the past. Technology will be available for everyone, and the differentiating factors will be the skills and creativity of the people using the technology.

In the next years, we will witness an accelerating shift in organizational dynamics and debacles from major organizations and even some countries.

The great enemy we are facing is inertia and the difficulty to reorganize and adapt companies to the new corporate realities and challenges caused by abrupt changes.

To conclude, here are the key trends for the next years.

Audience of the on-line media

The number of digital platform users will continue to increase and will be boosted by the following three factors:
- mass market broadband access
- growth of the "digital natives" generation
- the improving usability of applications and sites will support the growth of the population with access to the network on multiple platforms (web, mobile, consoles, netbooks, tablets, PCs, etc.), and an increase in the average time spent consuming on-line content and services.

On-line consumption via mobile devices (mobile phones and tablets) The new models are optimized for consumption, development and publication of contents on-line. Web traffic generated and the contents developed based on these devices will grow significantly in the next years.

Maturity of Web 2.0 / Social networks

The sustained growth of the social network audience is visible. And, as it has happened in the traditional media, social networks will also specialize. New social networks have emerged, segmented by topics (and groups within the "generalist" social networks), thus recovering the initial web 1.0 concept of Virtual Communities around thematic contents, behaviors, etc.

Cloud Computing

Companies and users will start using cloud computing services. The ecosystems that major world players (Apple, Google, Microsoft, Amazon, etc.) are creating are based on the "Cloud". Being able to access all information on any device, anywhere, will be a quick change process, both for individual consumers and for companies, with huge gains in terms of utilization and productivity.

Advertising / Marketing

The market share allocated to advertising and marketing in digital platforms will continue to grow strongly in the next years. The main reason for this growth has to do with the aforementioned growth of the audience and increasing usage time of these users, leading to an increasing investment of brands in the digital media, as we have been witnessing.

But in the coming years we will witness an increasing focus on the segmentation of campaigns, higher concern with the target audiences, and awareness and trust of the media where advertising campaigns are placed.

Segmentation according to the type of content/affinity and behavior (behavioral targeting) also will be the key variables in the planning of campaigns.

The richer formats (Rich Media), sponsored content and advertising in games (In-Game Advertising) will be the segments that will grow fastest. Brands will be increasingly focused since in these formats the reinforcement of brand awareness and trust by users has been proven.

For someone like me who fell in love with media, entertainment, communication and technology, this could not be a better moment to witness and participate in this new (Digital) Era. In these times of change, I feel privileged to be involved in and a witness to these moments in the history of humanity and the "daily pulse" of this Digital Era, still in the beginning.

References

(1) The Origin of Species
Charles Darwin - 1859

(2) Being Digital
Nicholas Negroponte - 1995

(3) Road Ahead
Bill Gates - 1995

(4) The New Socialism – The New Economy
Wired – Kevin Kelly – Junho 2009

(5) NetFuture
Chuck Martin – 1998

(6) Tracing the Evolution of Consumer Electronics. What's Next?
FastCompany – Julho 2009

(7) Social responsibility for free opinion making through new digital media?
Christian S. Nissen – Maio 2007

(8) Free
Chris Anderson – 2009

(9) The Long Tail
Chris Anderson –2006

(10) The future of the cloud – Computing at the horizon Dual Prespectives
Portfolio e Wired – Maio 2009

(11) How Gen Y & Boomers will reshape your agenda
Sylvia Ann Hewlett, Laura Sherbin and Karen Sumberg - Harvard Business
Review- – Julho/Agosto 2009

(12) e-Pub: une aventure de 10 ans
LeJournalduNet – 27 de Outubro 2004
http://www.journaldunet.com/0410/041027epub10ans.shtml

(13) Global entertainment and media outlook 2009-2013 – 10th annual edition
PriceWaterhouseCoupers - 2008

(14) Vendidos num ano 2,5 milhões de jogos
JN- Jornal de Notícias - 26 de Dezembro 2009
http://www.jn.pt/PaginaInicial/Tecnologia/Interior.aspx?content_id=1455714

(15) Analysis: Wii, DS Games Nearly Half Of 2008's U.S. Totals
GamaStutra – 26 de Janeiro 2009
http://www.gamasutra.com/php-bin/ news_index.php?story=21968

(16) 'Grand Theft Auto IV' sets record
Variety - 7 de Maio 2008
http://www.variety.com/article/VR1117985192.html?categoryid=18&cs=1

(17) Call of Duty: Modern Warfare 2 said to break sales records
CNet.com – 12 de Novembro 2009
http://news.cnet.com/8301-13772_3-10396593-52.html

(18) EA Acquires Facebook Game Maker Playfish For Up to $400 Million
Mashable – 9 de Novembro 2009
http://mashable.com/2009/11/09/ea-acquires-playfish-2/

(19) Electronic Arts Stock Evolution
Google Finance
http://www.google.com/finance?q=NASDAQ%3AERTS

(20) HUGE: FarmVille Maker Zynga Raises an Astounding $180 Million
Mashable – 15 de Dezembro 2009
http://mashable.com/2009/12/15/huge-farmville-maker-zynga-raises-an-astounding-180-million/

(21) Google Might Get Into Hosted Gaming Via YouTube
BNet.com- 29 de Dezembro 2009
http://industry.bnet.com/technology/10004543/google-might-get-into-hosted-gaming-via-youtube/

(22) Jogos que se pagam mais de duas vezes
DN – 19 de Novembro 2009
www.dn.pt/inicio/ciencia/interior.aspx?content_id=1424610&seccao=Tecnologia

(23) Um jogo com mais de 12 milhões de fiéis
DN – 19 de Novembro 2009
www.dn.pt/inicio/ciencia/interior.aspx?content_id=1424671&seccao=Tecnologia

(24) Videogame Advertising Engagement Study
Interpret / DoubleFusion– Julho 2007

(25) The 2009 UK National Gammers Survey
TNS and Gamesindustry.com – Julho 2007

(26) The profile of the European Videogamer
ISFE– 2007

(27) In-Game Advertising: Market Assessment and forecast to 2014
ScreenDigest/GroupM– Maio 2009

(28) Advertising Effectiveness In An Online Video Environment
Frank Magid Associates – Março 2009

(29) Marketing on the Internet
Jan Zimmerman – 2000 / Com Prefácio de Jerry Yang – fundador do Yahho!

(30) Leadership in The Era of Economic Incertainity
Ram Charan - 2008

(31) The world´s most innovative companies
FastCompany – Março 2009

(32) 10 Years After: A Look Back at the Dotcom Boom and Bust
Wired – 17 de Fevereiro 2010

(33) G.E. Makes It Official: NBC Will Go to Comcast
New York Times – 4 de Dezembro 2010

(34) The Wealth of Nations
Adam Smith – 1776

(35) Apple, Amazon, Google Wage Content Wars
As tech titans build incompatible ecosystems, marketers must rely on an array of devices—not just the Web—to deliver their digital messages
Business Week - 7 de Março 2010
www.businessweek.com/technology/content/mar2010/tc2010035_101984.htm

(36) Buffetology
Mary Buffet e David Clarck - 1999

(37) It´s now official: Apple is now worth more than Microsoft
Business Insider – 26 de Maio 2010
http://www.businessinsider.com/apple-worth-more-than-microsoft-2010-5

(38) Apple sells three milion iPads in 80 days
Apple – 22 de Junho 2010
http://www.apple.com/pr/library/2010/06/22ipad.html

(39) iPhone 4 sales top 1,7 million
Apple – 28 de Junho 2010
http://www.apple.com/pr/library/2010/06/28iphone.html

(40) iTunes Store Tops 10 Billion Songs Sold
Apple – 25 de Fevereiro 2010
http://www.apple.com/pr/library/2010/02/25itunes.html

(41) Confirmed: Apple Buys Quattro Wireless
Paid Content - 5 de Janeiro 2010
www.paidcontent.org/article/419-confirmed-apple-buys-quattro-wireless/

(42) iAd
http://advertising.apple.com/

(43) All Things D - D8 - Steve Jobs
All Things Digital - http://d8.allthingsd.com/speakers/steve-jobs/

(44) Apple COO Tim Cook: 'We Have No Interest In Being In The TV Market'
http://www.businessinsider.com/live-apple-coo-tim-cook-at-the-goldman-tech-conference-2010-2

(45) 2009 Brand Valuations
BrAND Z – Agosto 2009
www.brandz.com/output/
www.brandz.com/upload/brandz-report-2009-complete-report%281%29.pdf

(46) Google and HTC Working On a Chrome OS Tablet
Gizmodo – 2 de Janeiro 2010
www.gizmodo.com/5438716/google-and-htc-working-on-a-chrome-os-tablet

(47) Google and Partners Seek TV Foothold
New York Times – 18 de Março 2010
www.nytimes.com/2010/03/18/technology/18webtv.html

(48) KIN
Microsoft - 18 de Março 2010
www.nytimes.com/2010/03/18/technology/18webtv.html

(49) KINRIP
30 de Junho 2010
www.kinrip.com

(50) Microsoft MediaRoom
Microsoft - Junho 2007
www.microsoft.com/Mediaroom/WhatisMediaroom.aspx

(51) Nokia and Yahoo! to bring integrated web services to millions of consumers around the world
NOKIA – 24 de Maio 2010
http://www.nokia.com/press/press-releases/showpressrelease?newsid=1418261

(52) Nokia´s Plan to Rule the World
Fast Company – Setembro 2009
www.fastcompany.com/magazine/138/iphone-envy-you-must-be-joumlking.html

(53) Accenture Buys Symbian Services Unit From Nokia
InformationWeek – 17 de Julho 2009
www.informationweek.com/news/mobility/business/showArticle.jhtml?articleID=218501211

(54) Sony Reader, You Are So Dead
Gizmodo – 3 de Março 2010
www.gizmodo.com/5486667/sony-reader-you-are-so-dead

(55) How the Mighty Fall
Jim Collins – 2009

About the Author

Nuno Ribeiro

A manager focused on the business of media on digital platforms, Ribeiro has since 2008, been the director of the Multimedia Business of the Controlinveste group. Previously, he managed for eight years the Internet business unit of Cofina Media group, where he made economically feasible the digital projects of the publishing group. Between 1997 and 2002, he worked as a consultant to the Secretary of State of Social Communication for the digital area. He founded, in 1995, the website A Telefonia Virtual, that during the seven years of its existence was the reference for the Radio industry in Portugal.
He is an ambassador for Portugal in the only worldwide association of professionals and leaders in the operations and technology of on-line advertising – AdMonsters. He regularly writes opinion articles for Diário de Notícias and Meios & Publicidade.

Ribeiro holds a degree in Economy from the Catholic University of Lisbon, where he also completed an advanced course on Management of Technology Companies, as well as a post-graduate course on Media and Entertainment Management.

Blog: www.cibertransistor.com
Linkedin: www.linkedin.com/in/nunoribeiro